by the author

The Gathering (1965)
Please, Like Me (1968)
The Ends of the Earth (1968)
The Quivering Roadway (1969)
In His Image (broadside) (1970)

DAVID BROMIGE
THREADS

BLACK SPARROW PRESS
LOS ANGELES 1971

Thanks:
to the editors of these magazines where certain of these
poems first appeared:

CATERPILLAR
CHICAGO REVIEW
EPHEMERIS
IMAGO
IS
MADRUGADA
MEDITERRANEAN REVIEW
ROOTS FORMING
STONY BROOK REVIEW
SUMAC

to the National Endowment Fund

& to the Canada Council,

for time their grants afforded during

this book's composition.

Black Sparrow Press
P.O. Box 25603
Los Angeles, California

SBN 87685-020-4 (paper)
SBN 87685-021-2 (signed cloth)

for my father

Harold Bromige

Those chromosomes, I
yearned to be
as you, & you
delighted in
those anecdotes disclosing how
far you had grown from
Charley, him
who so closely, so
almost you
resembled.

Berkeley—Sebastopol, California
February 1969—June 1970.

CONTENTS

In His Image

"Having died
I was laid with eyes wide open in an open kind of grave
Tesselated marble, glazed
I gazed up at the sky
A stoned & Mayday gritty kind of sky

The camera stopped pretending to be me
It panned down, having drawn back
to show I lay, all senses but this vision numb, in a wide screen
of sky & tile, to reveal the aqueduct
(disused I guess) that held me up

Down, down, a long way, to the ground, no
to the river" a voice said
"The better the life he lived
the higher they raised him from the waters"

After the Engraving

(for Tom Clark)

What I am fashioning
with my light chisel
is an amulet to hang
round my love's neck

against disaster
dwelling in the hollows
well below, a spell
to keep the evil there

where she will never let me go
to fetch one home, to petrify
& carve upon, so I am making-do
by cutting-up an earlier craftsman's

amulet, & yet
it sets her loveliness off wonderfully
now it is done, & seems to
keep its charge, despite

the old man's admonition—
the old fool, for these meadows
to speak plainly, these haphazard
city streets, admit

of no surprise
to violate her pose
under our cool skies
woven of rocks soil & stones.

"What friends"

What friends came to be my comfort
I cannot name them all—Red,
Blue, Yellow

yet remembering you
I turned them away,
you would have known how to use them.

A Slot

Speak to the beautiful creature,
tell her she is so beautiful,

or how tired you've grown of dealing with her,
how, from the nothing left, you'll give her all.

First Love

(for M. H.)

I was angry because I'd had to wait
because we had missed connections
& meaning to meet in the heart of that city
that evening when we had been apart all day
because I had to have a job that kept me busy
& at the instigation of parties with our best interests at heart

because I was so in love with you I tortured
myself with thoughts of some utter misfortune
that must'v befallen you, for that would serve them right

& then, without you, fell into the pettiness
I'd been taught, of despising you because you couldn't
as I, so meticulously I could afford to be casual,
could, in this foreign setting where they lived,
find your way around.
                    So far north of home, midsummer, yet
dusk was in the village I had retreated to
searching for you, before I saw
the light glimmering of a garment & knew
in it, some summer fashion I guess they had afforded
for just such recognition as they feared, you were returning, safe
to my disappointment, your love, or mine
was for an instant such a burden, not safe?
to my joy.
             The old couple, old enough to be,
although they weren't, our grandparents
waited back at the cottage but
we strolled along the shore before we thought to
reassure them nobody had kidnaped &/or ravished
their niece,
              & kissed. The waves now breaking with a white
luminosity & a small
rain blew against us, but tomorrow
you would be gone, that made us freer
as in that american accent you acknowledged

13

promising always to be true to me as I
promised to be faithful too, the poor voices falteringly
meaning to write. I feel I've known you
all my life. & even though you
felt the mistakenness of it
we lay down & made love. Music through the squall
it seemed to us drifted
as an old air was driven
intermittently from the wooden
open dancefloor strung with fairy lights
where the local boats were berthed
where we had danced the night before that now
felt like so long ago,
that led us here,
polkas & schottisches that she knew
because she played the clarinet
back in Chicago, she'd shown, we'd looked together, at a photo
of herself in strident clothes, the uniform
of her high school band

back in Chicago, where two years later
I was to visit her
& where at last I lost track of her,
bank teller, harsh accents of the telephone
vanished even from the phone-directory
or/& into marriage possibly
or died, into America
where there's nothing now to say to her
who has, as anyone, her life to live

but I kept my vow to you
alive in every breaking of it,
in every desultory action felt as such
& still you visit me
with a kiss, as this, to give

whose particular form had never been
without her, we loved because of that.

Facing South

(For Gerry)

Creatures of insatiable appetites
devouring hamadryads themselves made of gnome-stuff
acting on the otherwise dead plant

to all intents & purposes, & showing how
to work those veins themselves
have set within the hill, this is a life

so self
referential that it seems a kind of hell
for when will one

come to set him free from gnomishness
unless he wear the clothes of gnomes
down to his very bones, but the Lady Belladona

until her end, has a skeleton whose skin
is a gauzey fluttering, to friend—
seeing which, I turn again

to the strange forms that pass
only to approach again tormentingly
enchanting me, to hell locked in

my element, & while that undine drum
upon the edge of things
thrums in my ears, I must aspire
above it, it & it, if only to make them mine.

The Quivering Roadway

only an illusion yet warning of the heat to be
prepared against, or for, that day
I locate you where you've gone to wander
under the dingy fir trees with the smoking
huts behind them, the ruined stalls, the creek
flowing past with a sluggish melancholy exactly
as befits a sluggish melancholy creek
as aimlessly as if, being a poet & lost
because your book was finished, you'd published it

yet forbore to take it seriously, how could you while
the husband, you couldn't remember
why you'd wanted, or he'd been forced on you, was off
like in the long-ships, at the war to elude us
he's waging over the dwellings where we might'v lived
because from his birth, those grooves in the heavens
had been manifest as soon as remarked on
& the good bright glint off their wolfram wings
Dum dum de dum dum.
                             I see the blistered torso
The limbs remarkable with bacterial action or
maggots, &, since a series of three
facts or whatever's most familiar to both our tribes,
the stillness of the woman, bare-breasted,
with her quiet
child clutched to her, sprawled in the tended yard

& turning, see you, or you, in the middle distance
where I suspect for some little while or lines
you've been attending, lift my eyes from
this vision & clearly
your appearance is distracting.
& behold that you are fair. Or
it's the intricacy of lines discovered
when your hem rides up, of the shining
dress, a gait elfin in its lightness
when the stockings whispering
asides to one another fix me
like a purpose, to possess

all in its very foreignness since I'm
in your sight, a mess, dwarfish
in all but stature, & so sincerely
anguished, yet articulate

—but yours is this difficult syntax
when you really want to be grappled with
I hear, disjunct as your body, mobile
limber but encumbered, as if the Mississippi
twisted through the versus of your flesh that bent
on postponing the sea,
                            the bright banality
of your conversazione like I
scream thick on apple-pie & like
some billboard pretending to be that, then
you giggle at the image yet
protect it. In your New
York or is it Okie
accent. I keep attempting
some quick
shift of the attention yet
you hold me, baffled
perhaps by the lack of anything intriguing where
beginning to make meaning out of tedium I hated
you. & my decision is made

plying you with gimlets till you slur the "t"
imploring me to take you home, no
not imploring, hinting, as I'd guessed
you don't want "involvement," just my body
being so unkempt & handy
As for yours, admiring your get-up I see
particularly when you adopt certain poses
an editor who's taken her pick
from various jet & hippie styles
but underneath the dross I guess
her beauty, & it's given me

One in a million, I say, one in a
million, you smile
                    of all the lustful studs in this tavern

to have the stripping of it from
a form they can only imagine, that dross
becomes a pleasure too. As if I read you
in a carrel, closeted above & under all those books,
the women at the neighboring tables send me looks
at that, conceit,
                        I take you underground, you notice is
simply a hotel room, whose bedside lamp
transforms to gold
down along the gloss of a body
to my astonishment, very much like mine
though fairer, to my ravishment, you want it off but no,
I have to wrestle, to shut your mouth's
inanities, with the light
hot flesh of my intent—Those bodies, you invented
just so's you could torture them
you charge me, without rancor, in fact
teasingly, Yes
maybe, but what is it
you want I ask, I won't discuss
what lies beneath contempt you answer
with the shadow of a sneer, cool fingers, one
cooler for its ring, begin
doing all that's necessary, & you finish

I don't give a shit about him either,
even while I grope within the red
gold tears you weep for him, opening
as though your feet rode in steel stirrups
& your syrups, intoxicating me, were of course
chemically given, to my reach

until at last in ecstasy you groan
& I have made you mine, or didn't I
groan, my cock's
rigidity phenomenal, as if of stone

that, flowing upward, takes my heart
yes, next my face, suffusing with it
Don't take it so hard you say but my mouth
has no words, your speech

echoes, back, from what you bend to read
but finds the runes predictably
indecipherable, & look so lost
in that instant I struggle to
speak of your fascination when you let yourself
look ugly?, no, defenseless

—but having got what you came or were called for
I'm left alone to witness
the woman playing with her child
beside their corpses, that you'd assured me were
mere words—her
impatient child, by the tension in these tendons
tearing at the features I now know
by a tenderness I can't suppress, as
those that so recently gave you back your own

now wandered on, by being motionless, beyond
earshot, wanting not
to remember the husband, whose bomb-sights, my
superiority to your indifferent back has pressed
my eyes against, use such stones
as this, we left, to find their target by.

Y

(An Imaginary Letter)

Dear Anon—we exchanged names but I never heard a word you
  uttered
to be honest, except Put some spit on it. I can't meet you
at the appointed hour tonight, is it
that the excitement is more than I
can stand, is even more intolerable when I think I will
than this hollow feeling, playing it safe?

You are preparing in our secret
rented room, in the next hotel we get to explore,
comparing fittings

because I will not name but touch
the gloss that bedside light predictably
lays on your hide, nothing is more naked
than the shoulders, but once begun

how should I stop now
seeing it all—your belly
white, flat
as a secret to one who isn't in it
& who doesn't care, but
I care, the crisp hair there

I stare, fixing the dim blue cords
that draw me so
back I almost tore this up, for you
must be the one to lay the vacuum
created by each undulating form eluding me
along the avenue beyond my knowing
for all the world as though I didn't know them
to be so similar each to each & you, so nearly
not totally particular in all their differences

but you, the thighs & only me between them, we are
& could be again together weren't we

& the hands, naked, now the rest's undressed
with the fingers that want to uproot me as I feel
your hands still
with the steel spikes straight through them—

                    *

—isn't the end of it, one evening
I'll find these metal pieces, with nothing but
what resembles rust around them &
discard them, then
it is the fingers will appear but shimmering
& this is why.

A Delivery

Enter, she laughed, If only you knew how
I've been expecting you, I said
Isn't that the very dress
you wore when last we met—

cut low over her breasts disclosing the flesh
for some dumb reason
she had refused on that occasion,
but she smiled now

& thickly whispered Yes
slipped out of it & in her nakedness
desirable as I had guessed so often
pressed herself against me

& truly flesh
of hers, as if there never
was any question but
what it always was

the answer granted me, was all
about me, & so fiercely
that I slept
lapped in the glow of a release

whose memory, when she awakened me
was so compelling I began
again to fondle her but she,
insisting I would be late

unless I got dressed instantly
wriggled away, though I was desperate
for joy, It's dawn, & time
I am to deliver you to

she added, The next woman
on this list in that
destination where she also has
been breathlessly

arranged since long ago she too
foolishly denied you
the permission
to a night as magical as this

alas now over—& a parting
since she like me
will have to drive you on
once it's done, at last as consummate

as this has ended.

For —

Four women in one day. Something
like satisfaction—so I don't care
that, for sure, it's not the world's record.
Close? Well . . . I enjoyed myself. Enjoy/d.

(Later). Complications
to be dealt with. (Later)

I wish I could burn out, if only for my poetry's sake
(this persistent sexual charge—it's tedious)
this sexual charge. What do I avoid,
by such activity, confronting.

But none of them was the woman
whose song must yet be sung
whose eyes, all pupils, as if they strain
to bring in all they can, whose eyes
or is it some expression of the face, that hungry
restlessness, that breathlessness
whenever we meet, that haunted me
as soon as seen, how could that be? *Whose* eyes—

who wouldn't fuck with me, or would, &
wouldn't, or circumstances, that had made all possible,
intervened, to make it not—somehow
both at once, naked
but with scruples, was I married then, was she

my wife's best friend? Or something stupidly
out of phase between us, as I bent
when she, being the girl she once was, involuntarily
drew me back, or being the child, bent likewise
so our skulls
struck, waking us up, or I passed out
because the liquor that'd let us kiss
then screwed me—stoned
& giggling, in the temple, at the notion that it is?
So even later, with the persistence of true love, in novels

24

together, late at night, a magic
lantern of a room, screening her eyes, the slide
of those thighs, net
stockings, no, yet some pattern, yes,
set, to be violated then, except
that violation made a pattern too, craving violation—

maybe I saved myself
(from what? what for?)
with intuition call it, suspecting that I couldn't
after, maintain distance, & how she
would despise me for my need—damn her despite, but that
it might cause her to deprive me of what then
I desired not to live without? Or wasn't it a hunch,
given her incessant list of conquests as they're called,
one man to the next, & women, she knew
I listened to, maybe she made some for no other cause—
maybe she didn't give a shit—some hunch

she was, if not frigid (but isn't that
a challenge?), then, congenitally
incapable of knowing when she'd had enough, mistakenly
taking her impulse, to be more, as sexual

always, does her allure
arise from this, when she enters the restaurant,
do I care? Shaking, thinking, not to shake, if I
possessed her once, ("possessed," we say)
would I be free—or by denying her myself,
as few men surely have, do I
lay this ghost, another way—

& either could be true, if I'd believe
one, wholly, but how can I, the distraction of those eyes
rendering belief impossible, except in them, that fact,
they're present—though they suggest
they're not, not wholly, they imply
other places, other times, all one can imagine
unimaginably re-aligned—I will

never have her,—or, I *shall*—
all this is previous to the fingers, tremblingly seized—
Enough
never to be mine,
but I have named the goddess
& in singing her refrain is all
the satisfaction I can know of her, as any man.

An Assignation

So you came back, who gave me a dose
& left on another's pillion—Pillow
Pillory Depilatory the triple
limits hidden I hear—hidden hair—

say you *are* an intention to play me false,
the force you play on to your end
stays true, although to save myself I would deny it—

hiding behind my fear of real potentialities
I've a mind to imagine, disease

domestic disharmony, mental dis
equilibrium,
                or my compassion
for my companion, or doesn't
that mean, merely, more quiet days for myself

—what does life care
for all my carefulness, what if
I wish you'd never crossed my path in words
now that you have

or if I flex my will tomorrow & don't go
to meet you as I did today,
"fail to show" they say,—they know
what they're saying
as do these words,—which would be sensible

in that act life is failed
though life is also this,
these thoughtful balances I must
one way or another act to
overthrow,
                & yet to save myself
from altering
I'd close my ears
to risk
becoming more myself,

nothing is clear but the force
that means I don't have to go it alone,
that makes me acquiesce or
in misery deny that it exists—

the bliss or misery I can't foresee
I'm certain of, the force
measured either way, where nothing can
protect itself, but life, to live.

The Guarantee

(for Andrew Crozier)

On Midsummer Eve 1969 3 men—blacks, as it happened—
came out of their car, or a car, toward me, & the one
who stood closest, asked me where Shattuck Ave, some
3 blocks off, was. As I began to answer he missed my
chin with a right hook but before I could move the one
who had come up behind me hit me very hard with something,
across the right cheek. While I yelled, all 3 dragged me
to the ground hitting & kicking me. What happened next
was, that, instead of killing me, they told me to lie
still & one tore my wallet out of my hip-pocket. With
the $15 & my I.D., they passed from my life. I walked
home, suddenly white.

Vengeance! quickly I grew sick & tired at the thought . . .
Yes, if it could be exacted up to one second *before* my
precious head was hit. Maybe what I'm about, now,
is a sort of revenge. They passed *into* my life. But the
gross literality of the tortures I'd imagined, their
vacancy, I want lost . . .

I'd known violence before naturally. The time, in the
taxi, with her straddling my neck, my head already out—
or when I found I'd thrown the cat across the room. He
limped always after that. Or limit it to midsummers—
she turned to me as I turned to her, my girlfriend's
friend: I shall never remember it right, it seems, nor
quite forget. I don't want to insist on my *sincerity*—
the words have a life of their own. Let's say, then,
it was she I married, though I can tell the difference
between one woman & another. But one carries shapes
within him. Look at all that's happened! & one could
say, that turned out very badly. I was often acutely
miserable & she was behind me all the way. I'd find
myself wishing I'd acted differently, trying to mend
my ways, but next night, there we'd be, at it again.

Dear Andrew, when you write, that much of my letter
to you, discussing poetry, is *unwarranted,* I hear it

29

as a question, one I'm unable to answer. But again,
I hear a voice, with all the decision an English accent
can suggest—that tone I've fled for most my life—
asserting a fact. But now it has happened, now my
letter has been born in your mind, & held you up—or
been assaulted—there, kissed, whatever the witness,
been wedded to if nothing else your disaffection, I can't
think, whatever you mean, that it is unwarranted, finding
your decisive word of closure revealing.

Psychoanalysis

Often people fuck merely in order
to keep from having to talk

but I don't remember everything
else I said.

You Too

I did just what I wanted to—
under orders once more,
& dressed in the uniform
I wore.

From Home So Far

How seldom I dream of my dead mother.
Of all the others . . . Her giant brothers—the six foot six
regimental sergeant major Uncle Walter, Walter
Cann, "water-can"
like the rest of those ten children of her, Ada's, mother,
Emma Balkwill, dead. But walk in dreams as memory—
how he terrified me—but not now. His absence
is more threatening. Do I imagine means to serve
what's gone the better not to come to some
donation of their remainder—"what's left over"—elementary
arithmetic, shit, it was all, even the deadliness, interesting—
invent, or, being over & over invented, by forces
they prevent me recognizing? I was late for the parade
he led, so I knew we were abroad, Brussels
the city of the pissing kid, or water-can (Water-loo—
posits a searchlight focussed on the center of one square
while the rest I consign to
whatever it was up to, what's Flemish for "fate"—the stories
        were,
it was early enough in the war—the Great—that, when in the
        end
he surrendered on behalf of what men he had left, the German
commander congratulated their gallant stand; &, he spent the
        next
4 years in Holland, p-o-w, subsisting chiefly on cabbage-soup . . .
& in 1945 my father was sent to Arnhem to direct a film
meant to account for the fuckup there, "Theirs Was the Glory";
he said the other day, The last time I saw it, I thought we overdid
the patriotism, I thought it dated. I guess I remembered
how proud I'd been, then, that my father made a film, a film
        of that,
for I felt desolate, when he said that.) "They died that . . ."

in *this* dream, Uncle only appeared on parade (one's penis
only comes to attention) outside England (trousers) & was the
        Queen's
representative on such occasions, though the resemblance was
        small . . .

the funeral of some soldier unknown to me, his small coffin
was in the barn. Borne there
by these distant relations . . . I wept
tears that left me helpless with pleasure as
sperm through the little slit when it's erect & stretched . . .

It Is Finished. (Emmanuel School.) (Dad,
visiting Berkeley, sleeps in the other room.) Leaving, I was
    hailed
by him, who, I realized, must'v all along been filming it,
he said nothing of my unexpected presence there
& grateful I offered to help him
& one other Gaumont cameraman—I think one
he had told me earlier, died in 1969—we had to port
a trough, awkward—I'm left-handed—filled with straw
& made of galvanized metal, wasn't it corrugated,
what does it matter—

he made me eager, or found me eager & developed that quality,
to help—& naturally,
what meant a lot to him supported me also, with various quirks
by way of qualification. (I said to her, As long as he's
in this house, I can never doubt each moment's charged with
    meaning—

but this dreaming was in a way better, being more my own
    thing,
or I was, more my own thing) That it became a pipe, a line he
    with
me was laying, through thick brush, the insects
thrusting up as emblems of another tale, helped here
by their mere presence, token of
the older metaphor for
the recent metaphor called "field," or
to say I don't get it all
isn't to say I don't get some of it, but
what? By what means, how given, turn it over, inspect it,
    searching
the silver cylinder for a manufacturer's sign . . . & finish your
sentence at the same time. "Sincerely yours, Morpheus." The pass
our task had brought us to was wooded, in a landscape

seductive & unending—the words
refer to pre-verbal images nonetheless post-verbal, since, last
    evening,
I had a vocabulary—yet are entities in themselves if I but let
    them
"take me"—who am I fooling?—seized
by my own head within its landscape! why not be

seized, what else so pleases, what can concern us but,
running from fuck to fuck, or dawdling along, secure that it's
    coming up—
or otherwise creating overruling passions
to disappear into—there were dizzy glimpses down, adjective
wedded to noun, despite the rules, language to mind despite
un wedded to consciousness, I didn't care
what was for tea, or if we missed it. Say
I was all the actual time lying
in a bed, asleep, to whom is this true
in the sense of verifiable? Or cryptically
select details of the bed & add perhaps recognitions of the room—
another mind makes something of them. Ceaseless activity.
The nub on the heather
carpet rucked up at one end. Or nap,—altering the rime-scheme
but admitting sleep. (At the party
300 attend, the understanding growing, like drunkenness, one is
replaceable—at least for all apparent purposes—no
one where to hook on, that doesn't frustrate equally essential
appearance of likely interest—turn em into zombies
to cheat, deny their demands. Preyed upon by zombies
then. & now.) (Tell the tale quicker—slower,
violate one's inbuilt sense of narrative, it's only narrative at all
because time teaches us such mode of apprehension,
longer, it takes longer to read,
instead of doing what
was so important, like picking up the kid
to teach it something unforgettable.) Cheat on the dream

one finds another form—it glinted
so I thought it an outcropping of some precious mineral but
a bottle, "poison," still half-filled—dropped
by the stranger. But then 5 of them, in polo-shirts & with $7

haircuts, multiplied are the divisions of my years, appeared,
single-filing, as close to lockstep as the terrain allowed,
I wouldn't tell my father, fearing he'd do some foolhardy thing,
bring the span to a premature end
with his insistence on getting it out in the open—

challenge the Mafia here with no-one to witness.
For this was their camouflaged factory-complex—
as country is
potential real estate—while opposite, against the sky
a garage became a motel of quiet but furious bustle
at the press of a button by this guy, alias
Mayor Alioto pacing its top walk,
genial, bland, assertive, & perfectly
communicating what he wanted to get over

—there was the matter of the train he'd purchased, Well
if we can make it run
efficiently—spoken as a joking sort of
vain hope, as if we didn't know
he didn't invest in a whole train for nothing, not even
if originally he'd been mistaken—it must work!
We'll rent it to Canadian Postal Service

Cann-Ada-ing my mother . . . Everyone vanishes,
the signs still flash
Lube Batteries No Vacancies

Parentheses: Mother—remember—Hello? (The party-line) . . .
I'm being a good boy, mum, or trying to—a real bastard.
Remember how we'd sit up late, you letting me talk on until
you'd say, Don't think so much, you'll go mad? Why
wasn't there anyone anywhere to teach me
since willy-nilly I began to think, to think! "Do unto others"
you said, & I did, & they did, orgies of incomprehension.
Distance
bleeding. Mother
sponge. Stop making those phrases you'll get stuck that way . . .
Nobody wants to go home, they talk of nothing else.
Because I have a hunch
in lieu of firmer knowledge such as

I am rambling on. Not sleepy. Tons of time.
(He makes $10000 p.a., pays $50 rent/month, & wonders
why somebodies don't do something for Biafrans. Does he send
money or stuff I asked but she hadn't thought to. How many
    families
would, say, $20 enable to survive—a while? The imagination
fails. Supposing he had died in his sleep . . . Whatever I say
dawn they call it breaks.) No man who isn't implicitly metaphysi-
    cal

picking his nose in a dark closet, while the world
holds his breath. Was my bladder full? Some kid,
in a yellow shirt, dashes by, admonished by his mobster father,
hidden by a factory doorway—in his chagrin the boy
didn't register our presence

but these 5 do, moving toward us without seeming to notice
they're remorseless
                        as, as leisure accretes, cultural lesions
will the Mafia be
moving in on Art? offing poets who move too fast—

But I clutched the phial to free myself from all coercion,
till like a parent it embraced its slave—too fast

So fast I didn't even know what hit me. Thrust by them in to
wakefulness—it feels

real good to be here, let
me tell
you, talking
& clambering up the gangway under the banana trees
to where I can
begin to see it all—as if I were the reservoir the pipe
should be connected to, as if I might
be my mother the night-mayor her majesty meaning
in terror of being her lover—

                    *

to end in the negative mode
faute de mieux & yet again
thereby obtaining absolution by cause of purposefulness

to play about with what I enjoy most of the time best—
or else I could describe this typewriter. Or tell the tale while I
    may
of a man with a name like her father, William Cann
A lad who came up from the country
to inherit a very large fortune & on only one condition,
that he pretend to be a famous person
who had died. Or rather, impersonate that dead man & foster
the illusion he's alive. The point was, I think

that he became even more famous than who he was meant to be,
as the truth leaked out, gradually,
this man who would lose all he had gained were he to be, openly,
even for an instant, who he felt he still must be—

& he suffered great anguish because of this sense of continuity.
He had devoted himself for three years to presenting
the image of the deceased, which was, of course,
another continuity, & well rewarded. Men of influence
& sexy women granted to his every utterance the force
which in truth was not his—or was it. This question
he puzzled constantly. He had lost all contact with
both mother & father. The bargain
at first had seemed advantageous, naturally, else he had refused
    it.
At last, desperate, he confessed the deception;
the members of the party where this happened
assured him that they had known for months,
but that they loved him not only nonetheless but exactly
because of his predicament. They advised
he do nothing about it. Everything is
poetry when you come right down to it, they said, What if
you're not the poet *he* was. It's simply different,
that's all, it lasts as long, & we can listen to it,
& welcome to the group. It's said
with this, everybody present rose,
& began to dance, which, in this place
was the customary procedure anyway. Later
they slept
in the house that kept its watch
by the strength of its construction, precisely.

"Why I went there"

Why I went there I don't know.
Dropping in unexpectedly like I did
where I've never felt sure of my welcome.
And an unfamiliar crowd—though I could be certain of two
bitches, who would put me down, if the opportunity afforded

but that Barrie should be there, his hand extended
& that in that greeting, ten years fell away
& that, though friends had told me, he'd grown fat
I was disappointed in that—yet prospering,
the guest of honor of a famous editor yet.

They all went on to another party leaving me
to look for you, way down on Grove, night
having come peculiarly early
& you were way past the time we had agreed on

to meet, in this district where just last week,
two acquaintances got beaten up

—this is all pretty straightforward, *you* stayed vague
as actual person, but the charge of feeling
allowable only when dreaming? like the turning of a head
once seen, giving all the dreck a commonality of meaning
—*you* were this composition of those loves, become my son
& the location of his kindergarden
& the fact of my separation from his mother
that keeps me here, where I can't find a job

accounts for the buried resentment, the barrier
—the heaviness man is. But that,
suspecting Barrie would now be alone
with that editor in his apartment
where the closest phone was, I might use
to call the cops, asking for news of you

& that, when I forced myself to go there,
this party was going on, & I forgot to phone

this is the essence, where mine
& the general nightmare mesh.

My Fault

You understood all about me & wouldn't
hear any different whatever the evidence adduced
against me, I loved you for that

if only that to myself I stayed so enigmatic,
that, in fact, in my confusion, sought you out—

&, apart from our arguments, that left me utterly
desolate, & you apparently
bewildered,
that soon passed, sooner for you
such was your love, happiness

was ours—I still see the cottage
with the tiny room, my study, with its roof
making it even cosier, sloping either way down to
thigh-level, so only an infant could'v stood
upright, at either wall, & its one window where,
struggling to get my understanding clear, I'd stare

out through the blossoms I always remember as being there
although we spent two winters in it,
at the large
mansion, only part visible, split into many
apartments, & glimpse
briefly this or that of its tenants, a few of whom we knew—

to cease these preoccupations, crawling in
beside you, in the room opposite, & in your arms
find sleep, a heavenly relief

godknows—where god is
the margin where
otherwise I might'v wandered alone, the name
given to all those
enigmas of disequilibrium summed
up for me in your laugh

remarkable in its assurance, if I was being stubborn
so sooner or later I could come around
to acknowledge my perversity
& you never bore me any grudge
that I could see, when gracious as that view
you opened up to me, who might show you who you were

so that we slept, you wouldn't take advantage of my rage
to treat me differently
so that I'd have to tear myself away from there.

Value

It would be best of all with a stranger

Best of all with the one you most love

As good with the one, as with the other
do you feel, it should be—

you want the unknown, or you fear it,
or fearing it, desire it, or
it's good because of that,

of the coming-into-being-known, of what,
before, was unknown, or
knowing once more, the known.

Did you forget her then,
wasn't she continually present,

everything must be *true*, right,
that is, whatever, there's
nothing more to say, or,

it would all depend on factors
omitted from this list, something

exceptional, or exceptionally
familiar, in the particular time,
that made it, more than the usual,
or different,
not less,

true, if the rest were lies, or,
if it weren't, then
otherwise, call it
what you choose, or
acknowledge, having to.

Paris in April

The intricate capilliaries
Speaking of pain in a relative way
As of joy naturally
Have come to say What else do you expect

As if that rhetorical flourish itself were
Its own justification in this place
Requiring none, a sudden blush
For embarrasment, a sudden pallor

For fear, of love
The face is a continuing brightness, a quick
Pulse, good muscle tone
Fed by the tortuosities encountered here

And known at all since they are close to the surface
Of things seen looking out
For themselves like a man looking at a woman
Steadily instead of at the pit

Of her stomach where the scars are staring
Into her eyes, nights
He will lie down in what
The day has given like a fridge a *Like*

Him to take his respite in
Tangled among those reflections
Of himself reduced he searches
Beside no other body for two gelid orbs

Where his poem properly should
End but for the grace
The body of that other visibly is
In place, whole as a world with its terrible history

No word can live
Without, like claws but only like
Her arms reach out
To us invisible to him

What else did he expect like the capillaries presented
Testify to a heart that's not
And though in her wholly he
Is "looking" in light's absence in her eyes

Acknowledged

There is a hero within me
who acknowledges only grim
necessity. When he sleeps

memories of men & women lost to me,
& children too, of the trust in their eyes
suffuse me, & stifling

our cries of joy at this reunion
we creep up to his room to smother him
but as his breath goes out

for the last time, each little light they hold
dies too, until no face
supports me in the dark I cling to

him in, hoping
against hope, but no, this once,
again, I suffer his embrace.

Fuck You

&, on that treadmill, the man
balked. Bribe me with torture or
implore me how you will, & whatever
I'm grinding out below

by those intricate devices I'll
know no more about
than the little I've found out, for all
—I'm through, A nous la liberté

his greatest of all cries
cut across the customary
hush of the internment
compound & the wheel, his share

of the intolerable daily labor, he'd
stopped stock
still on, halted, then rocked
back, before it also stopped, a fraction

& by just that much the wheel
whose teeth meshed through a six-foot slot
level with the ground, with his,
lurched forward, pinning her

body, he'd so often held to be his sole
consolation in the night's
propinquity, against the subterranean
cave's wall, caught off

balance while, as was her habit, lubricating
the hub to ease his task above
she loved, now all her pain
in shrieks ripped through the memory

of pain she had become incessantly
past rescue, while the cog
locking the trapdoor to her
cellar, failed to budge, locking the trapdoor too

to the tunnel lower, to the old
couple, so free
with their good counsel, You
must stand up yet, be a man

whose wheel
now unpredictably reversed & both
grew quickly faint, for want
of air, You are

burning it up too fast he swore, he tore
her dress, his present, as it happened, knotted a strip
& since persistently she gulped as if
adamant, began to throttle her—

while deeper yet, in a chamber gone
formless, with the settling flat
over the light-well, of one boss
projecting from the shaft that had,

revolving, served
to rock his crib, the babe
sobbed, waited, then
when still nobody came, began

to wail, & once more
faltering, stopped, fell
into a trance of hunger till
as he freely wept, his tears

gathering to a pool, bore up
what, minute, myriadfold
might swim
through it in a school

that one among them, maddened
by the sounds of agony
reverberating, split
away from, hurled

himself into her tiny
side, burying his head
as if a dart, therein
dying to kill the cries.

A Reflection

A continuity!—my son,
squatting on his heels,
when I come to pick him up from kindergarden

is so absorbed
in the picture he is painting I
sit quietly too, not to

disturb him, thinking
how I am absorbed,
& how the artist is

granted life again,
in him. Such moments are
timeless, one

says, later, thinking
of them,
gratefully.

"I can't read, & here's a book"

When I think my son says something like this
or this, when he's alone
I see him kneeling alone
in his room, sorting through what objects
choice & chance "conspire"

This is among the most poignant thoughts I know

The book I imagine is a 1945 edition
of Andersen's Fairy Tales
illustrated by Arthur Szyk

what makes me so uneasy, here, & why
am I driven to picture it?

How can I know
to what degree he is reflective,
what do I want of him. When he is
alone. When
I am alone. Thinking of him. When
I run out of
the particular kind of energy required
of me to be with him. & would sooner be alone
thinking, of him. However it hurts. Or soothes
what hurts. What displacing

makes him the book, while I am him?
How it feels, to be left out, closed out
of what all those others seem so vitally
to share.

How can I be witness to a scene
that, were I there, would be different again

There's nothing here
I can't ignore, for
it's only in my brain.

"They want"

They want objective criteria whereby to judge
their fellow members of the faculty. They say,
or one does, others nodding agreement,
We have numerous ways of knowing who, how,
someone is—student reports, other colleagues,
our own registrations, in class & out.
Somehow these delicate & complex means do not
suffice. But instead are to be funneled—
focussed—ordered, in, a form. As if prior
conclusions won't govern the way the categories
are responded to. The subtle is to be bartered
for the crude. Why—they want to hide behind
the form of the projected form, to escape the
consequences that the judgment is, one by one,
their own. They speak of the painfulness of
these evaluations. But also of the necessity
for them. The necessary pain, would be,
ameliorated for them by such a form. Is this
process much different from having an elected
representative, an "objective" argument, regular
rime-scheme, pretended structures to assimilate
& hide what's felt as the merely subjective?
One wants, then, to be relieved, of what he knows,
in all its consequence. One complication being,
this relief may bring release—of powers otherwise
not to be tapped. So I imagine their predicament.

"I can see"

"I can see arguments for both sides"
how impressive this intelligence
where will its weight be placed—
in this scale here
in that scale here

Midnight — "common sense" becoming its logic

(the document) Mental distress

that's not precisely it

Why would writing care anyway

(the writing) hang onto this—usually I'm ok
so in all likelihood I'll be ok tomorrow

What do I care about tomorrow
Then, what do I care?—Go on

The normalcy that makes this mood *aberrant*
would appear to be the guarantee of that

& is the measure of this present intensity,
those times, that is, when I don't see this clearly.

A passive voice—

adding up the calories,
a diabetic's necessity—
salmon, 1/2 cup, 100 of em,
couldn't have had more than that—
an egg chopped into the salad
begs to be remembered—

but *what about those dates*
I ate while waiting—

"the mind" is dodgy,
or, say, the habituation of it,
wants its hierarchies,
preserves itself,
even at the risk to the body of it
—except, I was enabled,
or is it, *able,*
to call those dates, "to mind."

Only Fair

But Lennie said he got it
so he should get half of it,
some 6 million lire. Only half

was for me to give to you. Later
I open up the banana
& it's rotten.

Precept

I've helped you in the past
Okay, go ahead, help me in the past again

Example

This burg isn't big enough for both of us
I just pulled the strings

"From some common model / blocking"

From some common model
blocking the harbor or
protecting it as if
some foundered vessel
we draw our sense of weaknesses,
but strengths of person too
to each are given,
                          along these
fault-lines let attention
as a chisel be driven
home, the stone
fracturing to portions one can lift
to live with,
                      in my mind
what insists on consistency
of imagery
breaks, making a rockpile of,
my home.

A Mystery

As for my face
I am less certain
when I see with what
assurance you wear yours

& the grace
difficult to attain I know
of all your motion
since they are human & you

as I am, a woman
inviting me to enter
the realm of such appraisal
emphatically as you

offer words, the food & implements—
didn't you sense then
in that instant clarity I'd gone
beyond, your furniture

become a bunker, no
an occult nest
wherein the worst
monster I can imagine

folded where I sat
into a mass less shapeless
than a ball, for all
your judgment rolls

impotently off
a thing so decidedly of
another kind, as it
would do, were I

able to be sure
my singular
being has beauty fed
by nothing more or less

than my steady
articulation of that fact,
a truth
endlessly hazardous,

even as yours
in yours
that shows me otherwise
yet I am sure in that.

Having a Thought

If I can only fake
an ambiguous enough
sequence of events in
here, maybe they'll be drawn

far enough into the light
these windows let onto the yard
to show me what
is going on out there.

Sides of an Intent

The cure proposed speaks chiefly of the individual
illness—the proposing is a symptom. The cure is
also in his care, a curate who needs souls to
authorize his assumption, of them. The syzygys
rule with their yoke. Kingship: freedom. Of women,—
here apparently, a farm of them. Fuck freedom:
so that there needs to be at all times a cunt present,
presented, to tell of, tell off, as if, being someone
who has to count, of crucifixion on mons veneris, of
monte cristo, ergo, one must have a cell, cut from
the rock with loving hands, to tunnel out of,—into.

Where it is dark, the blindnesses at least of epic
size. This realm requiring a firm hand at the helm
the hero wears in order to be clear about the also
necessary fog he thus prevents himself from knowing,
in order to have wrecks, rex, to be right.

Starboard. Starry-eyed—not blind but myopic, the key
to his hierarchical vision, close things clear, in a room
of dim ("fifth-rate") threats: the categorizing an
apotropaic act. Moving-away-from-meaning or -means,
where the self is inaccessible—shafted, say, walled-up—
into the resultant void rushes,—nothing, short of the
utter need to own, to own to, everything.

Everything comes attached to the time it unfolds in.
An impatient tapping out-of-time with his own reading:
can't wait to have done. The poem as means to an end:
applause, an applied mode of knowing one's success,-ion,
even the words get out of hand when the intent is to hold
them to one's rein. Slurred—drunken speech, drunkenness
would be a kind of health, whole with the near-blindness
otherwise so troublesome. One drink the means to, its
successor.

A life as a cry for surcease from a self that lurks in
such huge shadow; sticking its neck out hoping the head
will end on a pike,—how stricken with remorse they'll
all be then, for what they've done to me (they did to me
that, deprived of reflection, I bring to pass) &, peace
at last, from the body, from the head.

Being a Body

Guilty of loving another
woman than you are
the victim of my body is
this will as well that will
to win a race,
tax each ligament & muscle
looking for their limits
in the field, the undeniable
*

Certain inalienable rights
I wanted my love to be given you
but were they ever mine to give
if what you love is true
*

My body was never mine to give
but I was its, or I had never lived
*

I am my body's, then riddle me this sum:
my choosing you, my body's, everyone's.
*

I think we both
live in a fiction our bodies permit
demanding that we make it true,
or break from it
& make it true, & live the consequences
as anyway we do, however these demand
we punish it, the body
makes its own truth too, if these conflict
which of them said, there's any end to it.
*

Right now I love you & try
to make of that enough
a you who wonders who
to consider as
saying that I
makes its love.

Chris

I am holding the boy by one hand
I might call him my son
who I've just picked up from kindergarden
& there is this singing going on
inside or more of a happy kind of hum
right now, as I remember how
right then was now & then
I thought it, in words much like these
Well, something like
how I might call him my son
but I didn't think that made a difference
any more, this child I love
might'v been anyone, except, once
or actually for several months, he had to be
my son, or I wouldn't'v troubled to be close to him

& how, if it would make him feel good
even though it might be bad for him
I'd call him that,
& how there was noplace else I wanted to be
& nothing else I wished I was doing
though it's true I was feeling for this poem
& how there was nothing I could do about it.

An Imperfect Failure

There was no-one in the room above us
where the sounds came from, the one
within a minute of the other, that,
when we went up there, appeared to be
explained by your shoes lying as though
thrown, against the bedroom wall. We
had been talking in the living-room, you
while fixing some pretty christmas
decorations, taped to the windows, pictures but
non-representational—it was Bob
Stewart, who remarked, approvingly,
they were mandalas. Our marriage that'd been
breaking-up I had the day before announced
that I was leaving, the pain
& confusion intense, whether more guilt than actual
sense of loss impending or already
on us, or fear of loneliness or what, relief,
but pain, so much was clear—& that, each, again
had failed, in what each held, as we were trained, to be
of ultimate importance. One of the pictures
that shortly thereafter dropped to the floor
didn't get there, I think, because of a joint
para-psychic effort, a weak piece of tape
was more probably the cause. If a mandala
is what they claim it is it wouldn't matter that you didn't
recognize what you were buying—

how can I speak for you, but know myself
more fully alive, for that move
& the harm, maybe only of a different kind,
it inflicted on our son, & you,—or since that move, or since
not long before I therefore moved to make it

though explanations for all of it, like my guilt
trouble & elude me still, though
I have no mandala to round out my view
but this partial account my hunch says
has left much out, like broken pieces of plaster.

"Reassurance of his grunts"

Reassurance of his grunts,
heard while reading—grunts
suggesting understanding

or at least, some sympathetic
effort directed to that end—
then thinking Yes, but, it's only

him—how can he be thought
to be thinking for the others,
the ones I can't hear

grunting—all the while
I go on reading words
I've written, sounds

of some assurance
coming from
my mouth.

A Little History

Liberty—ME. & OFr. *liberte*
   L. *libertas* frm, *liber*, free

   ME. *fre, free;* AS. *freo,*
      not in bondage, noble, glad, illustrious

         Noble—L. nobilis, well-known, frm. base
            of *(g) noscere,* to know; famous, illustrious, renowned

            Know—AS. *cnawan,* akin to OHG. *cnahan;*
               IE. *gene, geno,* to know—"to have a clear
                  perception or understanding of"

         Glad—AS. *glaed,* akin to G. *glatt,* smooth;
            IE. *gladh,* shining, smooth—cf. GLABROUS,
            GLOW, GOLD

Free—IE. *prei,* to be fond of, hold dear, as also in Sanskrit
   priya, dear, desired, Eng. friend;
      basic sense of *free* probably "dear to (i.e. a kin
         to) the chief," hence "not enslaved"

Wherever you go, make friends with the cook
The illustrious cook, renowned for his glabrous puddings
Maybe some of his know-how will rub off on you
If you are smooth enough, if you know what you're about

You may get a lot of gold, or if you do not
You may be glad, your eyes will shine
Even though your skin may not be smooth
You may have something the others dearly desire
If they can't get it from the cook, you're made

Unless, understanding how to bash in a head
With a smooth stone, perhaps of gold, perhaps a famous stone
They bash in yours, perhaps friends, with their well-known kin
And when they perceive clearly what they have done

They'll be glad, wine & your blood will intermingle freely
Or if what they chiefly hoped to liberate is lost in your brain
Or even if not, they may have fond regrets, how noble
Their glow of remorse, as they turn on the cook
In their well-known way, their tears flowing this freely

At the Labyrinth

"Epistemology has traditionally aimed at defining truth
and falsity in impersonal terms, for these alone are
accepted as truly universal. The framework of commitment
leaves no scope for such an endeavour; for its acceptance
necessarily invalidates any impersonal justification of
knowledge . . . We may . . . represent a factual statement

from *within* as: $\left\{\begin{array}{l}\text{personal} \\ \text{passion}\end{array}\right. \longrightarrow \begin{array}{l}\text{confident} \\ \text{utterance}\end{array} \longrightarrow \left.\begin{array}{l}\text{accredited} \\ \text{facts}\end{array}\right\}$

and from *outside* as: subjective   declaratory   alleged
                     belief;   sentence;   facts.

*. . .The fiduciary passions which induce a confident utterance
are PERSONAL, because they submit to the facts as universally
valid, but when we reflect on this act non-committally its
passion is reduced to SUBJECTIVITY . . .* Any particular
commitment may be reconsidered, and this movement of doubt
would be expressed by passing from the first row to the
second; after which, having satisfied his doubts, the
reflecting person would recommit himself and move back
into the situation represented by the first row. But he
would find this return blocked if, having realized that
this movement involves an act of his own judgment, he
denied justification to it by reason of its personal
character.

In such case, the reflecting person remains faced with
the fragments of his previous commitment, etc."

Elsewhere in this compelling book *(Personal Knowledge)*
Michael Polanyi points out that "to speak a language is
to commit ourselves to the double indeterminacy due to
our reliance both on its formalism and on our own
continued reconsideration of this formalism in its bearing
on experience. For just as, owing to the ultimately tacit
character of all our knowledge, we remain ever unable to
say all that we know, so also, in view of the tacit
character of meaning, we can never quite know what is
implied in what we say."

*   *   *

Again, he remarks that "since the world, like a kaleidoscope,
never exactly repeats any previous situation ... we can achieve
consistency only by identifying manifestly different
situations in respect to some particular feature, and this
requires a series of personal judgments. First, we must
decide what variations in our experience are irrelevant
to the indentification of this recurrent feature," and here
I'm reminded of the poem I need but lack here, wherein the
unique event of *person* experiences similar singularities of
happenstance, unverifiable and hauntingly true, threads forming
a ghost to render the substantial world it hovers over
itself ghostly,—as in Heidegger's "wenn die Millionenzahlen
von Massenversammlungen ein Triumph sind—dann, ja dann
greift immer noch wie ein Gespenst über all diesen Spuk
hinweg die Frage: wozu?—wohin?—und was dann?"

There is an intense pleasure I experience in the juxta-
posing of the two polysyllabic words with the staccato
monosyllables—*greift* and *Spuk* particularly grip and
spook me. Doesn't all innovation in knowing happen much as a
pun: the thread of likeness enables one to articulate
what is in one sense the utterly dissimilar, since new.
Or what had been forgotten.

The News

A knocking making of itself attention
in myself, a stillness, entered by
groans, then a scream, from overhead, the bed

—the neighbor-woman coming
without intention to tell me something
until I'm filled with trembling

incomprehension I recognize so well
& back into the night go
sent, searching for you, myself.

"The length of the back"

The length of the back extending
in its peculiar slope below the almost
knobby, that protuberant, shoulders

into this poem & thus through time—
yet the poignancy it stirs in me,
how could *that* be here, unless

each time these lines were spoken they
disappeared into
                    thin air
by being there.

Choosing the Event

They want to be remembered for what they have done
as I was taught too, although we continue to live
but if you're an unlucky gambler
do you have to be a poor loser too? Why not
—"the bitterest men in the world—
they laid it on the line—
& nobody cares any more." Some D-Day hero
in the Chronicle because he had to
endure what he trusts never to endure again
doesn't want to forget the suffering
or does?
                    Or say you were on a rooftop
& in agony lost all you had
to lose—let's say because you wanted to be free—how,
if you're not past feeling now, do you feel
when others take upon themselves to speak to others
for you, interpreters
who negotiate your silence?
If they're mistaken, how to let them know—
if you are gone, who do they speak for
but themselves, thinking what they want
was what you wanted too
&/or are wanting still, freedom

to think for yourself & constantly
to change your mind, from any man's
over you, any man that enigmatic
we have to appeal to him
in phrases the helplessness of which that act reveals,
so that when your back is shot
& turned, the man can plant equipment in your car
making it all all right in San Fernando
while the living speak of death in vain, in vain.

In Time

At the last minute
it will come

yes, too late to prevent the unfolding
of events begun long before its arrival

yet as you're on your way out it'll fix you
with its radiance, so you will change your plans

to stay within its ambience
now that this place is

beginning to make such sense, you are afraid,
even though what now you've known

might reconcile you to departure,
the vulnerable one demands

that you survive, requires
all of your care,

yet don't you grasp, that it must go
on, beyond that possibility, twisted

past your recognition, if you
could be there, to witness—

what would your counsel anyway
have been, if time had granted—

for all your love
is the mystery, & strikes you dumb

explaining how to guard against
these gifts time rips from you.

A Man, Me

Say that I've sat
cracking sunflower seeds
hour after hour unable to stir

while the child I love lives
growing older a mere
six blocks from here—

say what was the kernel
insatiably I nibbled, the shells
littering the floor like cities black & dun

& if I went down on my hands & knees
under the right light, certain
works of art—or the impatience

when at last I saw the mess I sat in & leapt
up to sweep it all away or sat
down at this machine, to say.

A Providence

So the universe spewed us forth into itself
so we emerged out of that vibrato
like overtwanged elastic when I think about it,
space, time, epistemology

so strange-looking we are, the two of us
members of the cruellest species
crystallizing from   to-bear-each-other-company
"Why are you good to me" well, training

at or over the parental knee
nurturing in our patience what hostility
& will it erupt suddenly, or gradually
will you go to the Meninger clinic

& do I secretly wish it
since I managed to think it, wish it for myself
but lay it on you, is to disappear into the maze we came from
but if we touch, it vanishes

we're present—fostered by friends, like Bobby T
sleeping on the couch & you said You must'v been
dreaming—how could you be so sure, I wondered
looking around the room, if I expected

to find pieces of dream caught on the furniture
it's because you put that possibility there
& prior to that, those years
with the secret close focus of your eyes, & nest

of your hair, sometimes a fair
luminous cloud, sometimes I am not
allowed to read, & the manifold expressions
playful in your hands

your face your body you are
not all women, yet the thought appears
to contradict that fact—
I see the fragments we are

of the dream, of you & me
being in this room together,
what if this selfhood makes me tired,
I want to sleep.

3 Ways with the Same Sentence

I have striven for perfection
& still am permitted to sleep
on our mattress with its
broken spring next to the
completion of your body.

Not so much lately since
circumstance has seduced me
away from the initial fervor but
in youth as with a mission
I sought debauchery & remember
incidents of tenderness &
sanity that baffled me.

Godknows—god of my fathers
I have questioned all I could
yet still found means to live
when I woke up this morning nor
hold much hope things won't
once I am gone continue.

Logical Conclusions

If you went over to a friend's, a couple you know, say,
& knocked & knocked, & waited, the light was on, & then
knocked some more—& then
tried the door, so that it
opened, & you went in,
& found them sitting there. Would you want to stay.

If they leapt up & welcomed you, would you ever
trust them again.

Whatever it is

Art isn't the ultimate human act & for its sake I will
go blind & deaf & dumb, become a monster of denial.

An Answer

Touching your face with
wonder, sight less a blur than
a series of distinct
registrations, that close in,
yet skin, a
hovering kind of
color, knits the site together with
love, eye shines

I—a drag
back, down, felt in the solar plexus—
only a dream,
delusory, useless to ask these
questions when the mind
finds even its words this distant.

Two

Imprisoned within the liberty of a vocabulary
I yearn appears to be
one of those windows through whose screen
I see & it is glimpsed. Yearning to be

someone, a poet
in a poem, & knowing
no occasion short of his concerns,
supposing sometimes these are who he is.

Thus it is that through this life
one accompanies them as though a wife
yearning for divorce & hoping
for that once

again when truly one is wedded
& who can say the point of it
was the sexual embrace or that
she was the one embraced, nonsensical
alternatives, that utter sense, when split—

but that the moment of creation *is* its child
& if children are this issue
ranging through the world
this can't be the end,

knowing the so-called trivialities of marriage,
the bickerings & questionings
dispelling loneliness, stoking those fires, that blaze
to bliss shown forth for any
one to know, that *solitary, child*

appear to be necessities like this.

Fresh from Sleep

For*give*ness—what'd she
mean—that crazy lady.

I'd say this room's some 10 x 12 x 8.
960 cu. ft.
Just got up to blow my nose, so I paced it:
12, x, 14?—can't be sure—the bed + desk come
between me & one wall, & the wall opposite's
broken by a projecting closet. As for the height,
I still have to *assume* it's 8 feet.

Never knew it could be this cold in LA.

Do you think they'll be up soon.

I could use a cup of coffee—
I could use a holocaust.

My fault—took the coverlet off the bed last night,
"upon retiring," & hung it over the window
so's the next day, the light shouldn't wake me.
Woke about dawn, shivering.

What time is it.
5 cars have gone by already (quiet street).

Plenty to look at here—not like most bedrooms.
Obviously where they put the kids.
But I want to go for a walk, restless,
one window has a screen nailed over it,
the other, the one it'd be easier to go through,
onto the front porch, is painted shut.

Hill opposite—quite rustic, houses, shack-y,
"climbing" up it. Or I would. I can see what
looks like a chicken-shed—a poplar—6 fir trees
along its ridge—5 thin pylons with innumerable cables
(count em?) attached—a radio transmitter?
Can't hear a thing.

While I'm looking, 2 cars drive by. One a small
truck with mattress in back—
put me on it!

3.

Going to be a hot day, if I'm any judge.

I used to play the guitar once.
I tried, anyway.
Guess I should'v stuck with it.

Should I have read that poem—
the one about the man grunting during a previous
reading—so close to the beginning of
last night's reading.
I wouldn't read it at the afternoon reading.
Drinks, in between.

She looked like a nurse, by the shoes.
First pedestrian.
Waiting for the hospital bus, back in
North Battleford—
I *think* I know how it felt,
but if I recall the same time in another mood,
wonder.

Surprisingly few cars on the freeway between 5
-5.30 p.m., yesterday. S kept speculating
as to their whereabouts.
"The Martians have landed."

One
    of
        the
            kids
                just
                    had
                        a
                            piss
                                !

Could I tiptoe out without waking the others.
What about the dog.

Besides, I'm kind'v enjoying this.

This is a really nice block—
I can see how one wouldn't think so,
living here.

Where's the smog.

None even in Pomona . . . A pretty lady, that,
said I reminded her of her first love,
"But don't worry—you've established your
own identity."

Difficult to know what to say, to that.

Who was that, her husband wanted to know.
So did I, & I don't even know her.

Car stopping—negress, if one can say so,
Afro-American? a lady with dark skin—
just say, *a woman*—some loss of accuracy,
of actions upon any hearer's understanding—
in nurse's uniform—picks up 2 more—
for the 7 o'clock shift? You mean I only got
5 hours sleep?!

Too late now—2 more cars drive by.

3.

Robert Creeley showed me how supportive
this literal a selection might be—bless
him, whatever his intent. If *I* were sitting here,
writing, all you'd be hearing'd be pitiful rage.

Whoever you are, Bromige.

Speaking of seduction—

once I did, or was, by, with, such a lady—
nothing wrong with that. Play a movie of the
evening, see how it all cohered.
Stuck together I suppose.

Think I'll get up & walk right out there
& boil some water.

*

20 *to* 7! how'm I going to get through the day.
Wait & see.

At least, got a spoon—I can eat my yoghurt.
Smells better than it tastes. Have I carried it
around too long.

The girl, 7, 8, was awake, gave a big smile as I
tiptoed past.

Birds, for hours.
Fly away!

I don't really want to go for a walk.
I want S & wife to wake up & talk to me.

Let's see—3 kids, all school-age—
she'll have to be up by 7.30.
I could go for a walk till then.

What shall I say when I come in.

Forgive me.

An Interlude

No gap but these
threads in demonstrating
close, no strand there
but's anchored &
wilfully grasped
here, no ill
will dismissing this idea that doesn't
illustrate its truth,
I think, but gazing at this landscape each
choice has brought me to, whose wind
scatters my intention only to
secure me in another, hear
all borne on that air
allowing me to hear while sounds
conceiving others in the ear
knot up this will till I
too am a bead & what I have to say

*

Whatever opposites that correspond
to the dualism in each aXe
name them,

thread of my song
as if to reconcile
those *threats* she heard
where you belong

could help, for still
if in no other way
I could be wrong.

*

Let the epiphenomena
try to tell
its tale, to tell
its trials, its
prosecutor's name.

The Ends of the Earth

Always—that attraction
that I attach the word *love* to,
came before
whatever I explored—

whatever body, *hers* was there—
or *his*—or *mine*—

whatever landscape, *that* book
or friend had led me there, that *look*—

no idea I entered but what, first,
some *you* had fired me to,
no argument—no resolution

to have done with it, but love
had gone before.

Threads

it says, Are
parlous. A word
from the dead—

we have to wake him every 4 hours through this night
to check his balance & articulation. A heavy fall.
So senseless, stupid, its suddenness
stupefying. Reading to him from *The Princess & the Goblin,*
news to me too, a brilliant moon this night of open windows,
the traffic raucous up Cedar—

"When I please, I can make the lamp shine through
the walls—shine so strong that it melts them away
from before the sight, and shows itself as you saw it.
But . . . it is not everybody can see it."
"How is it that I can, then? I'm sure I don't know."
"It is a gift born with you. And one day I hope
everybody will have it."

Old privileges—old interferences with the authentic—
nor can I ignore these *golden* mists, *jewelled* crowns
& dresses, slippers *richly jewelled*—the calm parlours
of piracy. Nor that the grandmother's love, embracing
the mud-covered child, that is supposed to be proven
by her carelessness for her splendid dress, is qualified
when she knows all along that she can clean it with 3
passes of her magic coal—technology, & Victorian
hypocrisy.

Yet I yearn with belief, "born with you"—the child's
vision these o-so-knowing-ones I form my arguments among,
have had stripped from them, from me—"You must not
doubt the thread. Of one thing you may be sure, that
while you hold it, I hold it too." What thread

Immigrant into a time & place where the one fabric that holds
at all, demands its dissolution—member of an outworn
(threadbare) class, the power that was its virtue passed
into the corporations & their slaves

Would it be poetry, this evening my publisher phoned,
about our contract, & tales of faith betrayed by brother
poets, members of a small band rent by internecine feuds

each desperate—hot or determinedly cool, gritting his
teeth against caring—for his meanings, what thread
doesn't enslave one to its granted power—

& if the story we make of our lives—a warp of dream,
a weft of actuality—be the fabric of my soul—that
fabrication—there are days I lose the thread, when
pitiless duration's is the syntax—

however I talk to myself now in the ancestors' gift,
they are gone, their words . . . *Thesternesse* for instance,
an imagining of hell as dark, cold, outside

has now found the place it described

"I must confess that sometimes I have been afraid
about my children"

"it always takes the side of the thing we are
afraid of"

as if the dying light illumines this
fear, this thread I cling to
wind in to give courage
born of what fearful event comes next
we need to face

naming the unfolding invisible chord whose womb
enables us, by staying hid.

Age of Gold   (after Rimbaud)

Some one of these voices
all ways angelic
—where I am concerned—
quick as green is explicit:

These thousand questions
themselves ramifying
amount to what, in the end,
but crazy & drunk being;

recognize this shaft
so gay, so easy:
it's nothing but wave, flower,
& that is your family!

Then she sings. Oh
so gay, so easy,
& nakedly viewable . . .
—I sing with this she,—

Recognize this shaft
so gay, so easy,
it's nothing but wave, flower,
& that is your family! . . . etc. . .

And then a voice
—she is angelic!—
where I am concerned,
quick as green is explicit;

& sings on the instant
a sister of breath:
the tone is Germanic,
yet ardent with depth:

The world is vicious;
if that's news to you!
Live & leave to the fire
obscure misfortune.

Oh! charming château!
Your life is that clear!
Of what Age are you,
princely Nature
of our older sibling? etc...

Me, I sing along:

Multiple sisters! Voices
not at all public!
Enfold me
discreetly with glory ... etc...

from Memory   (after Rimbaud)

Sport of this eye of somber water, that here I cannot reach,
oh, little boat, immobile—oh, arms, too short! neither the one
flower nor the other: neither the yellow which importunes me
here; nor the blue, the beloved in the water color of ash.

Ah! the pollen of the willows which a wing shakes loose—
the roses of the reeds slowly, long since, consumed—
my boat, fixed still; & its chain straining
in the depths of this limitless eye,—in what ooze.

A Note on Translation

These versions: these two poems by Rimbaud have lost some of
their original resonance in being made mine—or say,
made over by me. I had no sense of egotistical
arbitrariness during this process, rather each poem
insisted on this particular sense being made of itself.
Of course this may be self-evasive. Familiarity with
the originals will at once enable another to recognize
them from my versions and to judge what liberties I had
to take.

That is the risk, *bien sûr* ... Despite the fact my saying so
argues otherwise, I am persuaded of my rightness, in them.
Living, one brings what's native into imitative play as any
child, & by the time reflectiveness is habitual, who is
to say where the line falls. He can't spend his life in
virtuous uncertainties—this translator whose every work is
original—or what is sureness for.

Still, Polanyi's series doesn't end with *accredited facts,*—
one will act upon such, like the woman next door who is buying
a gun for fear of "hippies," & the imagination supplies the
details, the stranger lost in the fog, knocks & gets shot ...
it hasn't happened. Yet *has,* already, in the world, that
measure of all possibility. I suspect that they are justified,
who argue we should live in the present, & wonder when
they'll join me.

The distal pistils/ this proximate ooze: yesterday I wished
for a tortoise. I seldom think of them. This was in the
morning & at noon a friend called, bringing a tortoise he had
just found. If *coincidence,* what can that word connote.

One wants to find out what he can do, what knowledge is
hidden in him. How am I tuned in, to Rimbaud. It remains then
to actualize his knowledge among his kind, & attend their
registrations.

Oh, it can be said, Glory is the aim. I don't see why not but
for myself believe I know why I am enamoured of what has been
forgotten. When I was two my parents sent me to an isolation
hospital fearing I had TB. Because, later, there was family
talk of this, I had that kind of memory of it, but had got it

into my head that I spent a week there. Two years ago my
father said, Oh no, four months. We weren't allowed to visit
you. I felt this accounted for much in my life that had
bewildered me. Say, then, I take this for my sign: as much
as that other, the instilled yearning to be helpful—
communal. In my own rages I know what force accumulates
to tear apart common fabrics when one has been "for one's—
for the family's—own good" suppressed. Then the hope is
to disturb assured minds helpfully. For this, one requires
contact with rigid thinkers. Probably oneself—my concerns
don't shift much. "Age of Gold" attracts me chiefly I think by
that canny refrain, that appears to be upset yet returns,
if on "other" lips, thus changed, again & again.

Man has this otherness, so that I imagine Rimbaud, the
failure to find a community, the loss sustained,
of his impatience. (Therefore *patience,*—no art sans that.)
This other is the imaginary act of one, too. But I don't
believe that's the end of it.

There is this Man, we make up.

An Invention

My moon being in Virgo, the date
(the given) of my birth, October
twenty-second—cusp of Libra,
yearning toward Scorpio

what is to become of me
if accident refuses   fatally to
intervene, might be determined
given the learning, the genes

wherein such fate lies coded
wait to be read,
dread
suggests one of the keys

which, if depressed, would make
its astral organ-pipe resound, allows
a free decision, some fresh
definition of these constellated signs.

The Cause

I dreamt last night that she was dead
& waking thought for the nine hundredth time
how I was left cold by her flesh
that years since made all my world to shine

so that my frozen glances at her presence
so cold they didn't register that fact
any time during this recent past we've met
melted me to tears thinking actually Never again

& how I could love her once more were she dead—
the causes for this divorce where once we wedded
I've thought to discover but even if I did
could never bring this hand to touch her

even if she would I should
nor is the pity of it all that interesting
nor that ashen campfires cause adventuring
or vice versa, one of love's nature's is this:

but that were she cold, in truth
how we might kiss.

                    *

I see I mean where our natures are supposed
constructed tight as a room whose house obeys its landscape
with events as angles carrying all into perspectives

what's done is walls of flesh I drive this nail in
to hang this picture of her from, & still my future grieving
The walls are gone, in truth, but still this feeling.

                    *

Old measures for my feeling, you are sources too
Such tenderness in the mind I find in lying down with you
to tickle my distrust—the man I have become
listens uneasily to his sentimental father's son

& shrewd, time
is the trap—what space

permits old loves & present to mingle
freely save this speech—what face

threaded, as though the thought is chromosomes
with all of meaning we have ever met
but this, & in its radiance
the single soul to save itself

dissembling, certain of utility
& bent on its true fate.

"Once. . ."

Once in a dream of Meaning Meaning drifting came
into a mise-en-scene I thought Saskatchewan
or thought some extra holding up a cue-card
that said it was, as in another part of Shakespeare

We rejoice for the brown grass or simpler,
the hour itself, the first flakes named at all
because they hint of a prior fall, the prairie
white with it, the soft inviting banks
beside where the hiway is becoming inaccessible.

The Reels

The sky ripped with winds
snagged on points of pine or fir
to spill its seed upon the snow but
deep below lay
rock, that fertile ground

that, with their great
Thaw, silted among marshes where
we stirred. But what about the blue
indifference far south—
into her mouth she gathered
heat spawned there, the white
witch, what if she drowned
at midnight, proving our
mistake, at the eleventh hour
our boundaries had burst—now
even the apparently
impermeable lead in sheets not broken by
the Beobab betrays—it is a screen

posited *the same* but
never seen unless a movie
flickers over it, yet posit
its reality one has to, plus
this cinema all fought to get
positioned in—didn't you
want to be thought
a mine of
information—yearning

after Europe, & the huge
images advance—

Asia, & it is
undeniable—

then say, is it the restlessness, this
insufferable sussuration of
the other customers, isn't it meant to be

free, crying for our money
back, Sit down
Stand up Go
home

—& the images
implore one, the spirit
thaws, the sky
washes to a pale
white blue about
black pupils the horizon
dances in, where in an elfish ring
with headphones senses
set up shop to soulfully purvey

certain elements long meant
for one's illumination

below a darkening sky.

"There are joys"

There are joys
luminous as the air when itself
is quick to replace what rises

rushing in against the direction of the sun
& endangering
so bellying the sails
the little boats

& joys
born of this force

Wherever I was banished I remember

you had loved me

I had been loved, love
a common term

& what was done, in its name
done for one's own good, & good
known
in its overwhelming

Never out of mind you moved
that secured
in your feeling
with its acts

so however dark it grew where I was sent
I couldn't lose your spoor,
nor my intent

to let you know what I had learned,
a joy
so full I couldn't wait

& turned aside, lay down

as though into an argument whose subject
        was to objectify my call
    you made,
            in dappled shade,
    in woods of words,
            with it

so that you were spared
            to live,
    to wander my imagination

crying for your son

    as for your death.

Fond

Love, since you come to these
lips so often, I try but fail
not to feel what you
can be, one
thread, I
think, maybe the strongest

of the many that prevent me
from dissolving utterly,
that night
when at last I was alone with what's
most dear to me, I
couldn't sleep because I had to
concentrate,

or because, relaxed, my mind was
freed to wander till it
lit, on a small
knob of metal in

the kitchen,
projecting, from the drawer
that keeps the knives
safe, while I can
concentrate.

"So"

So these were kittens, this the kittens'
basket was their bed, their
home, these eyes
looking back at his,
their eyes. The vowels
mesh with the consonants

& on that screen the words
form, *if I can concentrate*—
a pining, as if one might
crawl in among their number

to partake. But the assurance,
reprimanding one for his mistake,
is that voice I longed to join
mine to, that resonates

demanding that I get it right—
I hear it echo even in the slyness
when I disobey yet try
pretending to be good
as the iamb haunts these signs of feeling
I'd be mine: Write

how it is meant—
how are the kittens
meant to be, stripes
I remember, but that's a beating too, & rank—dapplings
as a general notion you
should see—he took the snapshot
fixing one instant

or my mother did, that, linked
making one time, moves, moves
me, with these, back-in-on-out-to
where but here consorting with
memories I'm sorted by, that happiness
that slumped
him, that boy, against that door,

found in a litter, though we say
lost, of these concentrated joys—

when they told him, drowned,
what explanation had they offered,
the farmer couldn't see the use of them—

his misery I think was twisted through with wonder
drawing him to words like death or loss
assunder with fresh life—

then the resentment, that he hadn't been allowed to
help, at what
he tried to figure out they hid with words—

Lots more cats come in a little while—

but never
these, not even
here, that's something else,

nor he
survive the general end to curl,
precisely so, in I again.

*Printed December 1970 in Santa Barbara
for the Black Sparrow Press by Noel Young.
Design by Barbara Martin. This edition is
limited to 1000 copies in paper wrappers;
200 hardcover copies numbered & signed by
the poet; & 26 lettered copies handbound
in boards by Earle Gray, signed & with an
original illustration by the poet.*

Photo credit: David Baker